PROVEN WAYS TO MAKE YOUR MONEY LAST:

A comprehensive guide for retirement

Audrey C. Washington

All rights reserved. No part of this publication may be reproduced, distributed or transmitted in any form or by any means including photocopying, recording , or other electronic or mechanical methods without the prior written permission of the publisher , except in case of brief quotations embodied in critical reviews and certain other non-commercial uses permitted by copyright law.

Copyright © (Audrey C. Washington), (2024)

About The Book

Proven Ways to Make Your Money Last: *A Comprehensive Guide for Retirement*

Are you prepared to enjoy the retirement you've always dreamed of? Discover the secrets to making your money last and secure your financial future today!

In a world where financial uncertainty is all too common, Proven Ways to Make Your Money Last: A Comprehensive Guide for Retirement by Audrey C. Washington offers you a roadmap to lasting financial security and peace of mind.

This book is not just another financial guide—it's a powerful, practical, and essential tool for anyone looking to maximize their wealth and ensure a comfortable, worry-free retirement.

What Makes This Book Stand Out?
Unlike other retirement planning books that offer generic advice, Proven Ways to Make Your

Money Last dives deep into the strategies that truly work, tailored specifically for today's economic realities. Audrey C. Washington, a seasoned businesswoman and expert in personal finance, business growth, and retirement planning, brings her decades of experience to the forefront, providing you with the knowledge and tools you need to take control of your financial future.

This book is packed with actionable insights, from setting clear retirement goals and building a sustainable budget to crafting a personalized investment strategy that balances growth and security. Audrey's clear, engaging writing style makes complex financial concepts easy to understand, ensuring that you're fully equipped to make informed decisions that will benefit you now and in the years to come.

Key Themes and Unique Selling Points:
- **Tailored Strategies**: Audrey C. Washington's advice isn't one-size-fits-all.

Instead, she offers personalized strategies that cater to your unique financial situation, helping you create a retirement plan that's as individual as you are.
- **Holistic Financial Planning**: This book covers every aspect of retirement planning, from budgeting and investment strategies to managing healthcare costs and adapting to changes in tax laws. It's a comprehensive guide designed to help you navigate every financial challenge retirement may bring.
- **Adaptability and Flexibility**: The financial world is constantly changing, and this book teaches you how to stay adaptable, so your retirement plan remains robust and effective no matter what the future holds.

What You'll Discover in This Book:

Proven Ways to Make Your Money Last provides you with a wealth of knowledge, covering critical areas such as:
- **Setting Realistic Retirement Goals**: Learn how to define and achieve the retirement lifestyle you've always envisioned.
- **Building a Sustainable Budget**: Master the art of creating and maintaining a budget that ensures your money lasts throughout your retirement.
- **Crafting a Secure Investment Strategy**: Explore investment options that balance risk and reward, tailored to your personal financial goals.
- **Navigating Tax Laws**: Stay ahead of changes in tax legislation and discover strategies to minimize your tax burden in retirement.
- **Managing Healthcare and Insurance Costs**: Get the tools to anticipate and manage healthcare expenses, ensuring they don't derail your financial plans.

- **Exploring Additional Income Sources**: Identify new ways to generate income in retirement, from part-time work to passive income streams.
- **Staying Engaged and Active**: Retirement is about more than just finances—learn how to stay physically, mentally, and socially active for a fulfilling life.

Who Will Benefit from This Book?
Proven Ways to Make Your Money Last is a must-read for anyone who is:
- **Approaching Retirement**: Pre-retirees who want to solidify their financial plans and ensure a secure future.
- **Already Retired**: Retirees seeking to optimize their finances, manage their wealth, and explore additional income opportunities.
- **Young Professionals**: Individuals early in their careers who want to build a strong financial foundation for the future.
- **Business Owners and Families**: Those interested in protecting and growing their

wealth for themselves and future generations.

Meet the Author:
Audrey C. Washington is a highly respected businesswoman with over twenty years of experience in personal finance, business growth, and retirement planning. Her passion for financial literacy and empowering others to achieve financial security has driven her to share her knowledge and expertise through this comprehensive guide. Audrey's practical, no-nonsense approach has made her a trusted advisor to countless individuals and businesses, and her insights are now available to you in

Proven Ways to Make Your Money Last.
Take Control of Your Financial Future—Order Now!

Your path to a secure and prosperous retirement starts here. Don't leave your financial future to chance—equip yourself with the strategies and insights that only Proven Ways to Make Your

Money Last can offer. Whether you're just beginning to plan for retirement or looking to refine your existing strategy, this book will provide you with the tools you need to succeed.

Buy Proven Ways to Make Your Money Last today, and take the first step toward a retirement filled with confidence, security, and lasting wealth!

Keywords: retirement planning, financial security, investment strategies, budgeting, tax planning, healthcare costs, income generation, personal finance, Audrey C. Washington .

About the Author

Audrey C. Washington is a distinguished businesswoman with a passion for personal finance, business growth, and retirement planning. With a career spanning over two decades, Audrey has established herself as a trusted advisor and advocate for financial literacy and empowerment. Her extensive experience in the business world, combined with her keen interest in financial planning, has equipped her with a unique perspective and a wealth of knowledge that she now shares with readers around the globe.

Audrey's journey into the world of personal finance began early in her career, where she quickly recognized the importance of sound financial management for achieving both personal and professional success. Over the years, she has helped countless individuals and businesses navigate the complexities of financial planning, from budgeting and investment strategies to retirement planning and wealth management.

Her commitment to educating others about financial stability and growth is evident in her writing. Through her clear, practical, and insightful advice, Audrey aims to demystify financial concepts and provide readers with the tools they need to take control of their financial futures.

In addition to her professional endeavors, Audrey is an active member of her community, frequently speaking at seminars and workshops on financial literacy and business development. She believes in the power of knowledge and is dedicated to helping others achieve financial independence and success.

Proven Ways to Make Your Money Last is a testament to Audrey's dedication and expertise. Whether you are just starting your financial journey or looking to refine your retirement plans, her book offers invaluable insights and strategies to help you make informed decisions and secure a prosperous future.

Audrey resides in New York City, where she continues to inspire and educate through her work and writing. When she's not busy advising clients or writing her next book, she enjoys spending time with her family, exploring new business ventures, and staying active in her community.

Introduction: Charting Your Financial Future

Introduction to Charting Your Financial Future

Imagine this: You're sitting in your favorite recliner, sipping coffee as the morning sun shines through the window. You've recently retired, and the world seems full of possibilities. You've worked hard your entire life, saved carefully, and now you're ready to reap the benefits of your efforts. But there's one nagging concern in the back of your mind: how can you ensure that your money lasts as long as you?

This isn't just a passing idea; it's a serious [1]problem for millions of retirees and soon-to-be retirees around the world. The concern of outliving one's savings is valid and pressing. After all, retirement should be a time for rest, leisure, and discovery, not financial stress and

---
1

uncertainty. That is where this book, "Proven ways to Make Your Money Last: A Comprehensive Guide for Retirement," comes in.

In the following pages, we'll go on a trip together to provide you with the knowledge and resources you need to make your retirement years as fulfilling and financially secure as possible. Whether you're just getting started with retirement planning, are on the verge of retiring, or are currently enjoying your post-work years, this guide is designed to provide you with practical guidance, actionable ideas, and confidence in your financial future.

The Importance of Planning

Retirement is more than just a stage of life; it is a momentous shift that necessitates careful planning and deliberate decision-making. It's time to shift your focus from accumulating cash to managing and spending it properly. The techniques that worked successfully for you in your working years—saving diligently and investing prudently—are still crucial, but they must be tailored to the specific challenges and opportunities of retirement.

Consider this: During your working years, you had a consistent paycheck, and your financial priorities were saving and expanding your nest fund. However, in retirement, that regular paycheck is replaced with a fixed income from sources such as Social Security, pensions, and retirement savings. This transformation requires you to be strategic about how you withdraw and manage your funds to guarantee they survive the remainder of your life.

Setting Retirement Goals
One of the first tasks on our journey is to determine what a successful retirement means for you. Retirement is a deeply personal experience, and everyone's idea of it is unique. Some may choose to travel the world, while others may prefer to spend more time with family, pursue hobbies, or simply enjoy a slower pace of life. Whatever your ideal retirement looks like, it is critical to have certain goals.

In this book, we'll help you define your retirement goals and develop a plan to attain them. We will help you examine your present financial condition, understand your retirement income sources, and develop reasonable, attainable goals. By the end of this part, you'll have a clear picture of your retirement goals and the steps you need to take to get there.

Developing a Sustainable Retirement Budget
A well-planned budget is one of the most important aspects of a successful retirement. This book will teach you how to establish a sustainable retirement budget that is aligned with your goals and allows you to live comfortably within your means. We'll lead you through the process of analyzing your expenses, identifying cost-cutting opportunities, and ensuring you have enough savings to cover the unexpected.

A smart retirement budget is more than just cutting back; it is about making informed decisions that will allow you to fully enjoy your retirement. We'll look at tactics for controlling significant expenses like healthcare and housing, as well as recommendations for keeping a balanced budget that allows you to live the way you want.

Smart Investing Strategies

Investing during retirement might be difficult. You need your money to grow, but it also has to be easily accessible and relatively secure. Balancing these demands necessitates a deliberate approach to investment. In this book, we'll look at smart investment ideas that help you attain both growth and security.

You will learn how to diversify your portfolio, balance risk and return, and choose the optimal asset mix for your needs. We'll give you tools to monitor your investments and make adjustments as needed to keep your portfolio on track with your financial objectives.

Navigating Tax Law Changes.

Taxes do not end when you retire, so understanding how tax rules affect your retirement income is critical. Changes in tax legislation can have a big influence on your financial strategy, so staying informed is essential for reducing your tax burden. This book will help you manage these transitions confidently.

We'll go over tactics for managing your withdrawals to reduce taxes, understanding the implications of required minimum distributions (RMDs), and taking advantage of tax-advantaged accounts. Mastering these concepts will help you keep more of your hard-earned money and make it last longer.

Managing Healthcare and Insurance Costs

Healthcare is one of the most significant retirement expenses, and planning for it is critical. In this book, we'll look at your healthcare alternatives, including Medicare and supplemental insurance, and present suggestions for properly controlling these costs.

We'll talk about how important it is to plan for long-term care and how to discover the best insurance policies for your needs. You'll learn how to select the best insurance plans, manage healthcare costs, and prepare for potential long-term care needs. Real-life examples and cost-cutting advice can help you negotiate this challenging element of retirement planning.

Exploring Additional Income Sources
Retirement does not necessarily imply the end of earning potential. Many retirees find joy and financial gain in seeking other income streams. There are many options to supplement your retirement income, including part-time work, consulting, and selling a passion. This chapter will look at many ways to make extra money, share success stories, and offer practical suggestions to motivate you. You'll discover how to use your skills and interests to build a fulfilling and lucrative retirement.

Staying active and engaged
Retirement is more than just financial security; it's about living life to the fullest. Staying emotionally and physically engaged is essential for a satisfying retirement. In this chapter, we'll discuss the significance of leading an active and

involved lifestyle. You'll discover a plethora of activities and volunteer opportunities to enhance your retirement years. Interviews with active retirees will provide motivation and practical advice for staying involved and enjoying your newfound independence.

Table of Contents
Introduction: Charting Your Financial Future

Chapter 1:
Setting Your Retirement Goals.

Chapter 2:
Building a Budget for Retirement.

Chapter 3:
Investment Strategies for a Secure Future.

Chapter 4:
Adapting to Changes in Tax Laws.

Chapter 5:
Managing Healthcare and Insurance Costs.

Chapter 6:
Exploring Additional Income Sources.

Chapter 7:
Staying Active and Engaged.
Conclusion

Chapter 1: Set Your Retirement Goals

Setting specific and attainable retirement goals is the foundation of any effective retirement strategy. Without clear goals, it is difficult to develop a financial strategy that provides a comfortable and meaningful retirement. This chapter will walk you through the process of selecting your retirement goals and reviewing your present financial condition so that you may lay a firm foundation for your future.

Understanding the importance of retirement goals.
Retirement goals are more than just financial targets; they include your preferred lifestyle, health concerns, family duties, and personal ambitions. Setting defined and realistic goals allows you to:

Clarify Your Vision: Determine how you want your retirement to appear, from daily activities to long-term goals.

Motivate Yourself: Setting clear goals helps you stay motivated and focused on saving and investing effectively.

Measure Progress: Setting specific goals allows you to monitor your progress and alter your techniques as necessary.

Reduce Anxiety: Knowing what you need to do alleviates uncertainty and tension about the future.

How to Define Your Retirement Goals

Visualize your ideal retirement.
- **Lifestyle Options**: Think about where you want to live (city, suburb, rural area), what kind of housing you like (owning a home, renting, retirement community), and your daily activities (hobbies, travel, volunteering).

- **Health and Wellness**: Consider how you wish to maintain your health and wellness, such as exercise routines, medical care, and psychological practices.
- **Social Engagement**: Consider how you want to stay connected with family and friends, community activity, and any new social circles you'd like to join.

Determine financial needs:
- **Basic Living Expenses**: Determine your monthly and annual expenses for housing, utilities, food, transportation, insurance, and healthcare.
  Discretionary spending includes expenses for travel, entertainment, dining out, hobbies, and other recreational activities.
- **Unexpected Costs**: Budget for unexpected expenses such as large house repairs, medical emergencies, or family support.

Assess your current financial situation:

To calculate your net worth, list all of your assets (savings, investments, and property) as well as your liabilities (debts, mortgages, and loans).

Income Sources: Identify all existing and possible income streams, such as pensions, Social Security, rental income, part-time employment, and investment returns.

- **Saving and Investing**: Examine your retirement accounts, savings, and investment portfolios to determine their growth potential and fit with your objectives.

Set specific and measurable goals.

- **Short-Term Goals**: Determine the goals you want to attain in the next 1-5 years, such as paying off debt, developing an emergency fund, or saving for a large purchase.
- **Mid-Term Goals**: Set goals for the following 5-15 years, such as saving a particular amount of money, reducing your home, or moving to part-time work.

- **Long-Term Goals**: Set long-term goals, such as earning a specified retirement income, maintaining a certain standard of living, or leaving a legacy for your descendants.

Prioritize your goals.
- **Essential Goals**: Prioritize goals that are critical to your basic requirements and financial security, such as healthcare, housing, and adequate retirement income.
- **Aspirational Goals**: Set goals that will improve your quality of life, such as travel, hobbies, and charitable contributions.
- **Adjustable Goals**: Identify goals that may be altered to reflect changing circumstances, such as discretionary spending and luxury purchases.

Developing an Action Plan

Once your retirement goals have been clearly established, the next stage is to develop an action plan to attain them. This involves:

- **Budgeting and Saving**: Create a budget that is aligned with your goals and highlights places where you can save more money or eliminate unneeded costs.
- **Investing wisely:** Choose investing techniques that are appropriate for your risk tolerance and time horizon, ensuring that your portfolio is diverse and growth-oriented.
- **Monitoring Progress:** Regularly assess your financial condition and progress toward your objectives, making adjustments as needed to keep on track.
- **Seeking professional advice**: Consider working with a financial advisor to get specialized advice and strategies based on your specific position and goals.

Setting your retirement goals is a very personal and important process that serves as the foundation for your whole retirement strategy. It's about imagining the life you want to live after retirement and then devising a strategy to attain it. This entails more than simply crunching numbers; it is about understanding what pleasure and contentment mean to you in your golden years.

First, you should consider your ideal retirement lifestyle. Imagine a normal day in your retirement. Do you explore the world, or do you prefer a simpler, quieter life closer to home? Perhaps you're pursuing hobbies and passions that you didn't have time for while working. Understanding your own goals is critical since they will greatly influence your financial demands.

Next, think about your health and wellness. Retirement often provides more free time, but it also requires the maintenance of physical and emotional health. Consider the activities that will keep you healthy and active, such as regular exercise, balanced nutrition, and mental stimulation from hobbies or continuing education. Health is an important aspect because healthcare costs are unexpected and may rise as you age. Planning for these things ahead of time will help relieve financial stress later on.

Your social life is another important factor to consider. Being socially active can have a significant impact on your happiness and mental health. Whether it's sticking near to family, reconnecting with old friends, or joining new community groups, these connections can have a significant impact on your quality of life. Consider how you will maintain and grow these relationships.

Once you have a clear vision of your ideal retirement lifestyle, you must convert that vision into financial terms. Begin by evaluating the expense of living your ideal retirement. This includes essential living expenses including housing, utilities, food, and transportation. Don't forget to account for inflation, which might reduce your purchasing power over time. Next, determine your discretionary expenditure on activities such as travel, hobbies, and entertainment. These are the expenses that will make your retirement joyful but are sometimes disregarded during the planning process.

Another key component is to **budget for unexpected expenses**. Life is unpredictable, and unexpected expenses might occur from medical emergencies, home repairs, or even providing assistance to family members in need. A contingency plan or emergency fund designated expressly for these events can serve as a safety net.

After evaluating your expenses, you should evaluate your existing financial status. Calculate your net worth by listing all of your assets and obligations. Your assets may include savings accounts, investments, real estate, and personal items. Liabilities may include any outstanding debts, such as mortgages, loans, or credit card amounts. Understanding your net worth provides you with a clear view of your financial situation and what you need to do to attain your goals.

Evaluate your revenue sources. For the majority of people, this comprises Social Security income, pensions, retirement accounts, and any other investments or savings. If you intend to stay partially employed or monetize a pastime, you should also consider part-time work or other income-generating hobbies. Make sure you understand the timing and tax consequences of each income stream, since they will influence your overall retirement income strategy.

To develop effective retirement goals, they must be detailed, quantifiable, and time limited. For example, rather than merely wanting to "save more money," set a goal of "saving $500,000 by the age of 65." Setting specific, quantifiable goals allows you to track your progress and stay motivated. It's also critical to prioritize your goals. Determine which goals are non-negotiable, such as basic living expenditures and healthcare, and which are more flexible, such as luxury trips or a second house.

The next stage is to create an action plan. This plan should detail how you aim to meet your retirement objectives. It covers budgeting, saving, and investment tips. Your budget should be in line with your retirement goals, highlighting areas where you may cut costs or save more. Investment strategies should be tailored to your risk tolerance and time horizon, ensuring that your portfolio is diverse enough to manage risk while pursuing growth.

Regularly tracking your development is critical. Life conditions and financial markets fluctuate, so you should examine your retirement plan on a regular basis and make adjustments as needed. This could include restructuring your financial portfolio, altering your savings rate, or rethinking your retirement date.

Consider obtaining expert help. A financial advisor can provide individualized advice based on your specific situation. They can assist you with making complex financial decisions, optimizing your investment strategy, and staying on pace to accomplish your retirement objectives.

By carefully defining and preparing your retirement goals, you lay the framework for a financially comfortable and satisfying retirement. This proactive strategy not only helps you attain your chosen lifestyle, but it also gives you peace of mind knowing you have a strong plan in place for the future.

Chapter 2: Budgeting for Retirement

Creating a comprehensive retirement budget is critical for maintaining financial stability and peace of mind in your senior years. A well-planned budget assists you in properly managing your income and expenses, allowing you to maintain your chosen lifestyle while protecting against unforeseen costs. This chapter will walk you through the steps of creating a solid retirement budget, including assessing your financial needs, identifying income sources, managing costs, and planning for contingencies.

Assessing Your Financial Needs:
The first step in creating a retirement budget is determining your financial needs. This includes calculating your monthly and annual spending based on your desired lifestyle and financial objectives. Your budget should include for necessary living expenses, discretionary spending, and any unexpected charges.

Essential Living Expenses

Essential living expenses are non-negotiable fees required to sustain your standard of living. This includes:

- **Housing**: Whether you own your home entirely, have a mortgage, or rent, housing expenses are likely to constitute a big portion of your budget. Consider property taxes, maintenance, utilities, and any homeowner association dues.
- **Utilities**: Utilities include regular payments for power, water, gas, internet, and phone service.
- **Food**: Grocery bills and eating out. As you age, your nutritional requirements may vary, affecting your food budget.
- **Transportation**: transit costs include the cost of owning and maintaining a vehicle, as well as the cost of using public transit or any other means of transportation.
- **Insurance**: Insurance premiums include those for health, dental, vision, life, and property.

- **Healthcare**: Healthcare includes out-of-pocket medical bills, prescription drugs, and routine health check-ups.
- **Taxes**: Keep track of property taxes, income taxes on retirement income, and any other taxes that may apply.

Discretionary Spending

Discretionary expenditure refers to non-essential expenses that improve your quality of life. This includes:

- **Travel**: Travel expenses include vacations, weekend excursions, and visits to family and friends.
- **Hobbies & Leisure**: Expenses for hobbies, sports, and other leisure activities.
- **Entertainment**: Entertainment includes movies, concerts, dining out, and other sorts of entertainment.
- **Gifts and Donations**: Make charitable contributions and give gifts to relatives and friends.

Unexpected Costs

It is critical to budget for unexpected charges, which might occur at any time and undermine your financial stability. These may include:
- **Home Repairs**: Significant repairs or improvements, such as a new roof or plumbing problems.
- **Medical emergency**: Medical emergencies are unplanned medical bills that are not covered by insurance.
- **Family support**: Family support refers to financial assistance for children, grandkids, or other family members in need.

Identifying Income Sources.
Understanding and maximizing your revenue sources is essential for creating a healthy retirement budget. Retirement income is often derived from the following sources:

- **Social Security**: Determine your Social Security benefits depending on your employment history and the age at which you intend to begin collecting benefits.

Delaying benefits can lead to greater monthly payouts.
- **Pensions**: If you have a pension, figure out how much you will receive and what payout choices are open to you.
- **Retirement Accounts**: Withdrawals from 401(k), IRA, and other retirement savings accounts. Be aware of required minimum distributions (RMDs) and tax implications.
- **Investments**: Investments include dividends, interest, and capital gains from stocks, bonds, mutual funds, and real estate.
- **Annuities**: Regular payments from annuities purchased as part of a retirement plan.
- **Part-Time Work**: Earnings from part-time jobs, consultancy, or freelancing.
- **Rentals**: Rental income is the money earned from renting out properties or making other real estate ventures.

Managing expenses

Effective spending management is critical for ensuring a sustainable retirement budget. Here are some techniques that will help you keep on track.

- **Keep track on expenditures:** Keep a careful account of all your expenses to uncover trends and places where you might save money. Use budgeting tools and apps to make this process easier.
- **Differentiate between needs and wants**: Prioritize important expenses while remaining wary of discretionary spending. To keep your finances stable, prioritize needs above wants.
- **Adjust spending**: Be adaptable and open to adjust your spending patterns when your financial circumstance changes. For example, if investment returns are lower than projected, you may need to cut your discretionary expenditures.
- **Optimize debt:** Before retiring, aim to pay off any high-interest debts. Refinance

or consolidate any remaining debt to save money on interest.

Planning for contingencies.
Preparing for unexpected circumstances is an essential component of a solid retirement plan. Here are a few strategies to help you prepare for contingencies:

- **Emergency funds:** Maintain an emergency reserve of at least six to twelve months' worth of living expenses. This reserve helps cover unforeseen expenses without jeopardizing your budget.
- **Insurance**: Make sure you have adequate health, dental, vision, and long-term care coverage. Regularly review your policies to verify they are still meeting your needs.
- **Estate Planning**: Write or revise your will, living will, and power of attorney. Consider establishing trusts or other legal arrangements to protect your assets and ensure your desires are followed.

- **Financial Cushion**: Set aside a portion of your savings to build a financial cushion that can withstand market volatility or unforeseen needs.

Monitor and Adjust Your Budget
Creating a retirement budget is a multi-step process. Regularly reviewing and updating your budget is critical to keeping it in line with your financial goals and changing circumstances. Here are some strategies for managing your budget:
- **Regular reviews**: Schedule regular budget reviews to keep track of your progress and make any necessary adjustments. Monthly or quarterly evaluations are advised.
  Adjust your income and cost predictions to reflect changes in your financial condition, such as changes in investment returns, inflation rates, or unanticipated expenses.
- **Seek Professional Advice**: Meet with a financial counselor to analyze your budget

and receive personalized recommendations. Advisors can help you make informed financial decisions.

Creating a retirement budget is a difficult process that takes consideration of both the large picture and the specifics of your financial situation. It's more than just adding up numbers; it's a planned strategy to ensuring that your money lasts throughout your retirement years while allowing you to live the lifestyle you want.

Understanding your spending patterns and behaviors is an important first step in creating a retirement budget. This insight stems from a thorough examination of your previous spending. Over time, analyzing your expenditure might show trends and habits that may persist into retirement. By reviewing previous bank statements, credit card bills, and receipts, you can have a clear picture of your spending on necessities and discretionary products. This historical data provides a framework for projecting your future expenses.

Forecasting is estimating how your spending will change in retirement. For example, some expenses, such as transportation, may fall while others, such as healthcare, may rise. Consider how inflation affects your cost of living. Even minor inflation can drastically reduce purchasing power over time, so it is critical to incorporate inflation projections into your budget. Inflation calculators and financial gurus can help you precisely predict these adjustments.

A key component of retirement planning is determining a realistic withdrawal rate from your retirement resources. Financial advisers frequently promote the "4% rule," which suggests taking 4% of your retirement savings each year. However, this is a general rule, and particular conditions can differ greatly. When deciding on a withdrawal rate, consider market performance, life expectancy, and unforeseen expenses. Flexibility is essential; being able to change your withdrawals based on economic conditions and your financial requirements will help you save your savings.

Healthcare is a major worry for retirees and must be properly incorporated into your budget. Medicare, while offering extensive coverage, does not cover all medical bills. Long-term care insurance is another option to explore, as it can assist cover the expenses of extended care services that Medicare does not provide. Early planning for future long-term care needs can help to avoid financial pressure later in life.

Housing expenditures can consume a significant percentage of a retiree's budget. Whether you intend to age in place, downsize, or relocate to a retirement home, you must first grasp the financial ramifications of each. Aging in place may necessitate changes to your house to accommodate changing physical needs, whereas moving may incur major costs involved with purchasing or renting a new residence. Consider the benefits and drawbacks of each scenario to make an informed decision that is consistent with your financial circumstances and personal preferences.

Entertainment and leisure activities can improve your quality of life in retirement, so make sure to budget for them. Whether you enjoy travel, hobbies, or social events, preparing for these expenses guarantees that you may continue to do what makes you happy. Furthermore, keeping active and socially engaged can benefit both your mental and physical health, thereby lowering long-term healthcare costs.

While it is critical to focus on creating a budget that meets your anticipated spending, it is also critical to plan for unanticipated financial issues. These could include economic downturns, tax changes, or unexpected personal expenses. Creating a financial cushion or contingency reserve can help you navigate unforeseen events without jeopardizing your financial stability.

Finally, ongoing education and adaptability are critical components of effective retirement budgeting. Financial markets and personal situations fluctuate, and remaining knowledgeable about them can allow you to make timely budget adjustments. Whether through self-education, financial planning seminars, or working with a financial advisor, remaining involved in your financial planning ensures that your budget remains current and successful.

Chapter 3: Investment Strategy for a Secure Future

Investing for a secure future is a multidimensional process that demands a combination of knowledge, strategy, and discipline. As you approach retirement, your investing plans must strike a balance between money preservation and growth. This chapter digs into the principles and methods that can help you achieve financial security by making wise investing decisions.

The first principle of successful investment is to identify your risk tolerance. Risk tolerance is a measure of your capacity to withstand market volatility without panicking. It varies from person to person, depending on age, financial condition, and personal character. Younger investors tend to be more risk tolerant since they have more time to recover from market downturns. However, as you approach retirement, money preservation becomes increasingly important, and a lower risk tolerance is frequently recommended. A thorough assessment of your risk tolerance aids in the creation of a portfolio that is consistent with your comfort level and financial objectives.

Diversification is a fundamental investment technique that helps manage risk. It entails distributing investments over multiple asset types, including equities, bonds, real estate, and cash equivalents. The argument for diversification is that various asset classes frequently perform differently under the same market conditions. For example, while stocks may be volatile, bonds may offer greater stability and income. By diversifying your investments, you can mitigate the impact of poor performance in a single asset class, improving the overall stability of your portfolio.

Asset allocation is strongly tied to diversification and is critical for reaching your investing objectives. It refers to the allocation of your investments across asset classes based on your risk tolerance, financial goals, and time horizon.

A well-thought-out asset allocation strategy can assist in balancing the needs for growth, income, and capital protection. As you approach retirement, one typical strategy is to transition to a more conservative allocation, increasing the share of bonds and other fixed-income investments while decreasing exposure to equities.

Choosing the correct assets for each asset type is critical. Diversification in the stock market, for example, should comprise multiple sectors and geographical locations. Investing in a mix of domestic and overseas companies can help you capitalize on growth possibilities while minimizing regional hazards. Similarly, in the bond market, it is smart to diversify your investments, including government, corporate, and municipal bonds, in order to distribute risk and maximize rewards.

Mutual funds and exchange-traded funds (ETFs) are popular financial instruments that provide diversity within a single portfolio. These funds pool money from multiple investors to buy a diverse portfolio of stocks, bonds, and other securities. They offer an effective approach to diversify without having to pick and handle individual stocks. Furthermore, ETFs often have lower expense ratios than mutual funds, making them an affordable option for many investors.

Rebalancing is another important part of keeping a stable investing strategy. Over time, market changes can cause your asset allocation to deviate from its anticipated path. For example, if equities do extraordinarily well, they may account for a bigger proportion of your portfolio than expected, raising your risk exposure. Rebalancing is the process of periodically changing your portfolio to bring it back into line with your initial asset allocation. This technique can assist control risk and keep your portfolio on track with your long-term investing objectives.

Tax efficiency is an often-overlooked aspect of investment strategy that has a major impact on net returns. Tax consequences change for various types of investment accounts, including taxable accounts, tax-deferred accounts (such as 401(k)s and traditional IRAs), and tax-exempt accounts (such as Roth IRAs). Understanding these ramifications, as well as strategically arranging investments in the right accounts, can help you save money and earn more after taxes. For example, putting high-growth investments in tax-deferred accounts allows them to develop without immediate tax ramifications, whereas putting tax-efficient investments, such as municipal bonds, in taxable accounts reduces your tax liability.

Income creation is a primary worry for retirees, who frequently rely on their investments to offer a consistent source of income. Dividend-paying stocks, interest-bearing bonds, and real estate investment trusts (REITs) are popular sources of investment income. Dividend and interest payments might provide consistent cash flow, whereas REITs generate revenue from real estate investments. To ensure that your portfolio meets your financial goals during retirement, you must strike a balance between the need for income and capital preservation.

Annuities are another way to generate money in retirement. An annuity is a financial contract that offers a series of payments at regular intervals in exchange for an initial investment. They can provide a guaranteed income stream, which is especially useful in reducing longevity risk (the danger of outliving your resources). However, annuities can be complex and come with a variety of fees and conditions, so it's critical to understand the terms and compare possibilities before deciding on one.

Inflation protection is crucial for long-term investors, particularly retirees. Inflation gradually erodes the purchasing power of your money, and failing to account for it might jeopardize your financial stability. Investments in assets that have historically outrun inflation, such as stocks, real estate, and inflation-protected instruments (such as TIPS), can help preserve your purchasing power.

Including these assets in your portfolio can act as a hedge against inflation and assist guarantee that your income stays up with rising expenses.

Finally, being educated and seeking professional guidance is critical to understanding the complexity of investing. The financial markets are dynamic, and staying up to date on changes in economic conditions, tax regulations, and market trends can help you make more educated judgments. Working with a financial advisor can provide significant insights and individualized recommendations based on your specific situation. An advisor may assist you in developing and implementing an investing strategy, monitoring your portfolio, and making changes as needed to stay on track with your financial objectives.

Investing for a secure future is an ongoing process that involves careful planning, constant monitoring, and the ability to respond to changing circumstances. Understanding your risk tolerance, diversifying your investments, strategically allocating assets, and being educated can help you develop a strong investing strategy that will support a secure and satisfying retirement. This proactive approach not only helps you meet your financial objectives, but it also gives you piece of mind knowing that your investments are working hard to ensure your future.

Investing for a secure future necessitates a sophisticated combination of strategic vision, adaptability, and a deep understanding of market dynamics. Aside from the fundamental principles of risk tolerance, diversification, and asset allocation, there are several layers of strategic planning that might improve financial stability.

One such layer is the consideration of various life stages and how your investing strategy should adapt accordingly. Early in your career, the emphasis is frequently on growth, with a larger tolerance for risk in order to optimize returns over the long term. As you amass money and enter mid-career, your strategy may evolve to a balance of growth and stability, aiming to protect your gains while also exploring prospects for significant returns. In the pre-retirement and retirement stages, the approach typically focuses on capital preservation and income production while maintaining a lower risk profile to hedge against market volatility and assure a consistent cash flow.

The macroeconomic climate and market conditions also have an impact on investment strategy. Economic cycles, such as expansion, peak, recession, and recovery, can affect the performance of many asset classes. Being aware of these cycles and altering your investment mix accordingly can help you increase profits while reducing risk. For example, during an economic downturn, it may be beneficial to allocate more assets to defensive sectors such as consumer staples and utilities, which are less affected by economic slowdowns. In contrast, during periods of economic boom, increasing exposure to cyclical sectors such as technology and consumer discretionary might result in better returns.

Technology and innovation play an increasingly important part in investing strategy. Technological improvements have democratized access to information and trading platforms, allowing regular investors to execute tactics that were previously reserved for institutional investors. Algorithmic trading, robo-advisors, and automated portfolio management systems provide advanced tools for optimizing investing decisions, lowering expenses, and improving portfolio performance. Staying educated about technological advancements and incorporating these tools into your investment strategy might provide you a competitive advantage.

Environmental, social, and governance (ESG) parameters are increasingly important in the investing landscape. ESG investing entails making investment decisions that take into account a company's environmental effect, social responsibility, and governance procedures. This strategy not only corresponds with ethical principles, but also reduces the hazards associated with unsustainable activities. Companies with good ESG performance are frequently better managed, more resilient, and well-positioned for long-term success. Incorporating ESG aspects into your investment plan can boost both financial returns and beneficial societal effect.

Global diversity is another important component of a sound investment strategy. By distributing investments across multiple countries and regions, you can reduce the risks associated with economic and political instability in a single market. Emerging markets, for example, have significant growth potential but more volatility. Developed markets are more stable, but may have lesser growth possibilities. A well-balanced global portfolio can capitalize on growth opportunities while minimizing exposure to region-specific dangers.

Alternative assets, such as private equity, hedge funds, commodities, and real estate, can help diversify your portfolio and generate additional returns. These asset classes frequently exhibit little correlation with traditional equities and bonds, providing opportunities for higher risk-adjusted returns. However, they also carry distinct hazards and complications that necessitate careful consideration and skill. Working with individuals that specialize in these fields can help you understand the complexities and optimize the benefits of alternative investments.

Financial education and literacy are critical components of successful investing. Understanding financial concepts, market dynamics, and investment products enables you to make informed decisions while avoiding typical errors. Continuous learning by reading, attending seminars, and interacting with financial experts can help you improve your investment skills. Furthermore, encouraging financial literacy in your family can help future generations manage and increase their wealth.

Behavioral finance is a growing discipline that investigates psychological influences on investment behavior. Emotions, biases, and cognitive errors can all contribute to poor financial decisions, such as panic selling during market downturns or following trends without proper scrutiny. Understanding these behavioral inclinations and employing tactics to limit their impact, such as establishing predefined investment guidelines and keeping a long-term view, can lead to better investment outcomes.

Philanthropy and legacy planning are critical components of a holistic investing strategy, particularly for those with significant wealth. Establishing charitable foundations, donor-advised funds, or endowments can help you achieve your philanthropic goals while also delivering tax benefits. Legacy planning is arranging your inheritance so that wealth is transferred efficiently to heirs and beneficiaries, while also ensuring that your financial legacy reflects your values and supports future generations.

Navigating regulatory and legislative changes is another important aspect of investing strategy. Tax laws, banking regulations, and government policies have a substantial impact on investment returns and tactics. Staying up to date on regulatory developments and collaborating with tax and legal experts can help you optimize your investment plan and assure compliance.

Chapter 4: Adjusting to Tax Law Changes

Adapting to changes in tax legislation is an essential component of financial planning and investment strategy. Your financial landscape can be substantially influenced by tax laws, which are dynamic and can affect everything from income and investments to estate planning. It is imperative to maintain a state of informedness and adaptability in order to optimize financial efficiency and reduce tax liabilities. This chapter explores the strategies and factors that are essential for adapting to the changing landscape of tax regulations.

Various factors, such as changes in government policies, economic conditions, and political agendas, can result in the modification of tax laws. These modifications may include the introduction of new tax rates, the modification of rules regarding retirement accounts, investments, and estates, and the alteration of deductions and credits. It is imperative to be proactive in comprehending and adapting to these changes in order to preserve financial stability.

Staying informed is one of the initial stages in adapting to new tax laws. This entails the consistent consultation of reputable tax information sources, including the Internal Revenue Service (IRS) website, financial news publications, and professional tax advisors. Subscribing to newsletters or alerts from trusted financial and tax organizations can help ensure you receive timely updates on legislative changes. Professional organizations, such as the American Institute of Certified Public Accountants (AICPA), also provide essential insights and analysis on tax law changes.

Working with a qualified tax professional is invaluable when navigating changes in tax laws. Tax advisors and Certified Public Accountants (CPAs) are endowed with the knowledge and expertise to interpret complex tax regulations and their implications for your financial situation. Regular consultations with your tax advisor can help you understand the nuances of new laws and develop strategies to adapt accordingly. Tax professionals can also help identify potential tax-saving opportunities and ensure compliance with the latest regulations.

Proactive tax planning is essential to effectively respond to changes in tax laws. This entails reviewing your financial situation and making adjustments to optimize your tax position. For instance, if new tax laws introduce higher tax rates for certain income brackets, you might consider strategies to defer income or accelerate deductions. Deferring income can be achieved through methods such as maximizing contributions to retirement accounts or timing the recognition of capital gains and losses.

Retirement accounts are often affected by changes in tax laws, making it important to remain updated on new rules and regulations. Contributions to traditional retirement accounts, such as 401(k)s and IRAs, are typically tax-deferred, meaning you don't pay taxes on the contributions until you withdraw the funds in retirement. Changes in tax laws can affect contribution limits, required minimum distributions (RMDs), and the tax treatment of withdrawals. Staying informed about these changes can help you make informed decisions about your retirement savings and withdrawal strategies.

Tax-efficient investment strategies are also crucial in adapting to changes in tax laws. Different categories of investments are subject to varying tax treatments. For example, long-term capital gains and qualified dividends are often taxed at lower rates than ordinary income. Understanding these distinctions can help you structure your investment portfolio to minimize taxes. Additionally, new tax laws may introduce or alter tax-advantaged investment options, such as municipal bonds, which are typically exempt from federal income taxes and may also be exempt from state and local taxes.

Estate planning is another area significantly impacted by tax law changes. Estate taxes, gift taxes, and generation-skipping transfer taxes can all be affected by new legislation. Estate planning strategies, such as creating trusts, making lifetime gifts, and utilizing the estate tax exemption, should be reviewed and adjusted in response to changes in tax laws. Regularly revising your estate plan with the guidance of an estate planning attorney can help ensure that your assets are protected and transferred according to your wishes while minimizing tax liabilities.

Tax laws also influence charitable giving strategies. Charitable donations can provide significant tax benefits, including deductions on income taxes. Changes in tax laws may affect the value and schedule of these deductions. For example, if new legislation increases the standard deduction, it might reduce the number of taxpayers who itemize deductions, potentially impacting the tax benefits of charitable contributions. Staying informed about these changes can help you optimize your charitable giving strategy to maximize tax benefits.

Tax credits and deductions are essential instruments for reducing tax liability. Changes in tax laws can introduce new credits and deductions or modify existing ones. Staying updated on these changes allows you to take advantage of new opportunities to reduce your tax burden. For example, tax credits for energy-efficient home improvements or deductions for educational expenses can provide valuable tax savings. Understanding the eligibility requirements and documentation needed for these credits and deductions is crucial for effective tax planning.

Income shifting strategies can also be beneficial in adapting to changes in tax laws. This entails transferring income from high-tax-rate entities or individuals to those in lower tax brackets. For example, you might consider gifting income-producing assets to family members in reduced tax brackets or establishing family trusts. These strategies require careful planning and compliance with tax laws to avoid potential penalties and ensure that they achieve the intended tax benefits.

Another essential consideration is the potential impact of state and local tax laws. Changes in federal tax laws can often prompt adjustments at the state and local levels. Understanding the interplay between federal and state taxes is crucial for comprehensive tax planning. Some states may conform to federal tax changes, while others may implement different rules. Staying informed about state-specific tax laws and consulting with tax professionals familiar with your state's regulations can help you navigate these complexities.

In addition to proactive planning, it's essential to maintain accurate and organized financial records. Detailed records of income, expenses, investments, and charitable contributions are crucial for tax reporting and compliance. Keeping comprehensive documentation can also help you substantiate deductions and credits in the event of an audit. Utilizing tax software or working with a tax professional can help ensure that your records are accurate and up to date.

Finally, maintaining flexibility in your financial plan is vital for adapting to changes in tax laws. Tax laws are subject to change, and new legislation can be enacted at any time. A flexible financial plan allows you to modify your strategies in response to new regulations and optimize your tax position. Regularly reviewing and updating your financial plan with the guidance of a tax advisor can help you stay prepared for changes and ensure that your plan remains aligned with your financial objectives.

Adapting to changes in tax laws is a complex and ongoing process that requires vigilance and strategic adjustment. The landscape of tax legislation is perpetually evolving, influenced by political shifts, economic conditions, and societal needs. For individuals and businesses equally, staying ahead of these changes is crucial for financial stability and growth.

One approach to navigating the fluidity of tax regulations is to cultivate a proactive mindset toward tax planning. This involves anticipating potential alterations and considering their implications well before they are enacted. By doing so, you can make informed decisions that align with both your current financial situation and prospective future scenarios. For example, if there is talk of impending changes to capital gains tax rates, you might evaluate your portfolio to decide whether selling certain assets now or later would be more beneficial.

A significant aspect of adapting to tax changes is comprehending the broader economic context in which these changes occur. Tax laws are often modified in response to economic conditions, such as recessions or periods of growth. For instance, during economic downturns, governments might introduce tax relief measures to stimulate expenditure and investment.

Conversely, in times of economic prosperity, tax rates may be increased to manage inflation and redistribute wealth. Recognizing these patterns can help you anticipate and prepare for shifts in tax policy.

In addition to federal tax laws, state and local tax regulations play a crucial role in your overall tax strategy. States have varying tax policies that can substantially impact your tax liabilities. For example, some states have high-income taxes, while others have none. Understanding the tax landscape of the states where you live and work can help you make strategic decisions, such as where to establish residency or locate your business. Furthermore, maintaining abreast of changes in state tax laws ensures that you remain compliant and can take advantage of any new tax benefits or credits that are introduced.

The international dimension of tax planning is also increasingly essential in a globalized economy. For individuals and businesses with international interests, changes in tax treaties, foreign tax credits, and international tax regulations can have profound implications. Staying informed about these developments is essential for optimizing your global tax strategy. For example, changes in international tax laws could affect how foreign income is taxed or how foreign tax credits are applied, impacting your overall tax liability. Engaging with international tax experts can provide valuable insights and help you navigate these complexities.

Another critical consideration in adapting to tax law changes is the impact on estate planning. Changes in estate tax laws can substantially alter the strategies you use to transfer wealth to your heirs. For instance, adjustments to the estate tax exemption limit or changes in gift tax regulations can affect how you structure your estate plan. Regularly evaluating and updating your estate plan in light of these changes ensures that it remains effective and aligned with your goals. This might involve revising trust structures, updating beneficiary designations, or contemplating new gifting strategies to minimize estate taxes.

Tax law changes also have implications for retirement planning. Modifications to the regulations governing retirement accounts, such as 401(k)s, IRAs, and Roth IRAs, can impact your retirement savings strategy. For example, changes to contribution limits, required minimum distributions (RMDs), or the tax treatment of withdrawals can affect how you save and withdraw funds for retirement. Staying informed about these changes and adjusting your retirement plan accordingly can help you maximize your retirement savings and minimize taxes.

Additionally, adjustments in tax laws can influence charitable giving strategies. New tax regulations may alter the tax benefits associated with charitable donations, affecting how and when you donate. For example, changes in the standard deduction could impact whether you itemize deductions and, consequently, the tax benefit you receive from charitable contributions. By remaining informed about these changes, you can adjust your charitable giving strategy to maximize tax benefits while supporting the causes you care about.

A long-term perspective is crucial when adapting to changes in tax laws. While it is essential to respond to immediate changes, it is equally important to consider the long-term implications of your tax strategies. For instance, making decisions based solely on short-term tax benefits could have unintended consequences down the line. A comprehensive and forward-looking approach ensures that your tax strategies are sustainable and aligned with your long-term financial objectives.

Moreover, technology and digital tools are becoming increasingly essential in tax planning. Advances in tax software and financial technology provide new methods to track and analyze your tax situation, automate tax filings, and identify tax-saving opportunities.

Leveraging these tools can enhance your ability to adapt to tax law changes efficiently and accurately. For example, using advanced tax software can help you model different scenarios and comprehend the potential impact of tax law changes on your financial situation.

Fostering a collaborative approach to tax planning is essential. Engaging with a team of specialists, including tax advisors, financial planners, and estate attorneys, ensures that you have access to diverse expertise and perspectives. This collaborative approach enables you to develop a comprehensive and integrated tax strategy that addresses all aspects of your financial life. Regular meetings with your team can help you stay updated on tax law changes, assess your strategies, and make necessary adjustments to remain compliant and optimize your tax position.

Chapter 5: Managing Healthcare and Insurance Costs

Managing healthcare and insurance expenditures is an important part of financial planning, especially as healthcare costs continue to climb. Whether you're planning for yourself or your family, knowing how to navigate healthcare systems, maximize insurance coverage, and budget for future medical bills is critical for financial stability and access to vital care.

Healthcare bills can be among the most substantial and unpredictable expenses you will encounter. To effectively manage these costs, you must have a thorough awareness of your health insurance alternatives and how to use them effectively. There are several types of health insurance available, including employer-sponsored plans, individual plans, Medicare, and Medicaid. Each type of insurance has different perks, limitations, and cost structures, which might affect your overall healthcare costs.

Many people and families obtain their health insurance through their employers. These plans are often less expensive than individual plans due to employer contributions and group rate negotiations. However, it is critical to thoroughly research the specifics of your employer-sponsored plan, including as premiums, deductibles, co-pays, and out-of-pocket limits. Understanding these aspects will allow you to plan ahead of time for your healthcare bills.

Individual health insurance policies are an option for those without access to employer-sponsored coverage. These plans are accessible through health insurance marketplaces established by the Affordable Care Act (ACA) or directly from insurance companies. When choosing an individual plan, you should examine coverage levels, rates, deductibles, and provider networks. Using resources like the ACA marketplace can help you choose a plan that fits your healthcare needs and budget.

Medicare is the principal source of health insurance for people over the age of 65. Medicare is divided into several parts: Part A (hospital insurance), Part B (medical insurance), Part C (Medicare Advantage), and Part D (prescription drug coverage). Each component addresses a distinct facet of healthcare, and understanding how they interact is critical for cost management. Additionally, many Medicare beneficiaries choose to acquire supplemental insurance (Medigap) to cover expenses not covered by standard Medicare. Carefully analyzing your Medicare alternatives and supplemental plans can help you reduce out-of-pocket expenses.

Medicaid is a combined federal-state program that provides health insurance to low-income individuals and families. Eligibility and benefits differ by state, so it is critical to understand the precise laws and coverage alternatives in your state. Medicaid can be a vital resource for people who qualify, offering comprehensive coverage at a low out-of-pocket cost.

In addition to choosing the correct insurance plan, effectively managing healthcare expenditures requires understanding and utilizing preventative care services. Most insurance plans offer preventive care at no additional cost, including immunizations, screenings, and wellness check-ups. Using these services can help spot health risks early, lowering the need for more expensive treatments later on. A healthy lifestyle, including nutrition, exercise, and regular medical check-ups, can help to reduce healthcare expenditures by preventing chronic illnesses and increasing general health.

Prescription drug expenditures can be a considerable portion of healthcare spending. To manage these costs, you must first understand your insurance coverage for prescriptions, including formularies, co-pays, and recommended pharmacies. Shopping around for the best costs, utilizing generic prescriptions whenever possible, and looking into prescription discount programs can all help you save money on your medications. Furthermore, several pharmaceutical companies provide patient assistance programs for people who cannot afford their drugs, allowing for further savings.

Managing healthcare costs can be especially difficult for people who have chronic illnesses or require continuing medical care. Creating a detailed care plan with your healthcare practitioner can aid in treatment coordination, reduction of service duplication, and cost management. Care management programs offered by insurance companies can also give assistance and tools for properly managing chronic diseases.

Long-term care is another important facet of healthcare planning, particularly as you age. Long-term care services include nursing facility care, assisted living, and in-home care for people with chronic illnesses or impairments. These services can be very expensive and are usually not covered by ordinary health insurance or Medicare. Long-term care insurance can help you protect your money and possessions by providing financial coverage for these expenses. When contemplating long-term care insurance, it is critical to understand the coverage options, such as benefit amounts, elimination periods, and inflation protection, to ensure that the policy matches your requirements.

HSAs and FSAs are useful instruments for controlling healthcare costs. HSAs are offered to those with high-deductible health insurance plans and provide tax breaks for saving and paying for eligible medical costs. Contributions to an HSA are tax deductible, grow tax-free, and can be withdrawn tax-free for qualified expenses. Many businesses provide FSAs, which allow you to set away pre-tax funds for medical expenditures. While FSAs include a "use it or lose it" clause, which means that funds must be spent during the plan year, they nevertheless provide a tax-efficient option to control out-of-pocket healthcare expenses.

Understanding and negotiating medical bills is another critical component of healthcare cost management. Medical billing can be complex, and errors are prevalent. Reviewing your bills carefully, ensuring that charges are correct, and understanding your insurance coverage can help you avoid overpayments. If you receive a hefty medical bill, don't be afraid to negotiate with healthcare professionals or seek help from a medical billing advocate. Many suppliers offer payment plans or rebates for quick payment, allowing you to save money.

Telemedicine is a growing trend that can assist reduce healthcare expenditures by giving easy and affordable access to medical treatment. Telemedicine services enable you to consult with healthcare providers remotely, generally for a lesser cost than in-person visits. Telemedicine for routine treatment, follow-up appointments, and minor health issues can save time and money while still providing quality care.

In addition to these techniques, it is critical to prepare for unforeseen healthcare expenses. Creating an emergency fund exclusively for medical bills can provide a financial safety net in the event of an unexpected health crisis. This fund should be kept distinct from your other emergency funds and easily accessible when needed.

Finally, remaining informed about changes in healthcare laws and regulations is critical for efficient cost management. Healthcare policy is susceptible to change, and new legislation may affect insurance coverage, pricing, and available benefits. Keeping track of these developments and knowing how they effect your healthcare alternatives will allow you to make more educated decisions and adjust your strategy accordingly.

Managing healthcare and insurance expenditures necessitates a thorough awareness of the different elements that affect medical spending and coverage. Beyond the fundamental strategies, it is critical to investigate advanced ways and lesser-known alternatives to improve your healthcare spending.

One critical factor to consider is the network of healthcare providers covered by your insurance plan. Insurance plans usually divide providers into network tiers, with pricing differing dramatically between in-network and out-of-network options. Choosing in-network suppliers allows you to take advantage of negotiated pricing, resulting in significant savings. However, it is critical to be aware of the possibility of requiring specialist care outside of your network, as well as to comprehend the cost consequences. In such circumstances, coordinating care through your main physician, who may assist referrals within the network, can help you save money.

Preventive services also play an essential role in lowering long-term healthcare expenses. Beyond basic preventative care, enhanced screenings and wellness programs provided by insurance companies can detect potential health issues early on, avoiding costly procedures later. Participation in wellness programs is frequently rewarded with financial benefits, such as decreased premiums or rebates, which can further reduce your overall healthcare costs. Furthermore, engaging in preventive care measures such as regular exercise, good food, and stress management can enhance general health while decreasing the frequency and severity of medical problems.

Another option to consider is integrating technology into healthcare management. Health apps and wearable devices can monitor a variety of health metrics in real time, allowing you and your healthcare providers to make more informed decisions. These technologies can monitor vital signs, physical activity, and other health parameters, allowing for early detection of potential problems and more individualized treatment regimens. Furthermore, several digital health platforms provide virtual consultations, saving time and decreasing the need for expensive in-person visits.

Understanding the complexities of billing and coding in healthcare can result in big savings. Medical billing errors are prevalent and can lead to overcharges. To avoid overpayment, familiarize yourself with common billing codes and ensure that your bills appropriately reflect the services obtained. Working with a medical billing advocate can help detect and challenge inconsistencies in complex medical procedures or treatments, ensuring that you only pay for what you receive.

Disability insurance should also be considered while developing long-term healthcare financial plans. Disability insurance protects your income if you are unable to work due to illness or injury. This sort of insurance is especially useful in managing healthcare expenditures since it ensures a consistent revenue stream to cover medical expenses and other financial responsibilities during periods of disability. Evaluating different disability insurance policies and knowing their terms and benefits will help you select a plan that meets your needs.

Healthcare financing solutions, such as medical credit cards or loans, can be effective cost-management tools, especially for unexpected or high payments. These financing options typically have lower interest rates than regular credit cards and can be used to pay for a variety of medical services. However, understanding the terms and conditions, like as interest rates and repayment schedules, is critical to ensuring that these options are used properly and do not cause further financial burden.

In the context of aging and healthcare, it is critical to investigate community-based programs and resources that can give assistance while lowering costs. Many cities provide programs that help with medical transportation, home healthcare, and access to affordable pharmaceuticals. These programs can greatly reduce the cost burden of healthcare, especially for seniors and people with chronic diseases. Engaging with local community organizations and government agencies can help you find resources and programs that are suited to your individual needs.

Those managing healthcare bills on a fixed income, such as seniors, should look into supplemental income options to help offset medical expenses. Part-time work, freelance possibilities, or passive income streams, such as rental income or investments, might help supplement healthcare bills. Balancing these revenue opportunities with the requirement to maintain health and quality of life is critical for long-term financial success.

Finally, advocating for legislative changes and participating in healthcare advocacy can help with long-term cost management. Individuals can help the larger community by supporting policies that aim to lower healthcare costs, enhance transparency in medical billing, and increase access to affordable treatment. Engaging with advocacy groups, attending public forums, and staying current on healthcare policy developments are all methods to help shape a more equitable and economical healthcare system.

Managing healthcare and insurance costs requires a complex approach that extends beyond basic tactics. Individuals can better navigate the complexities of healthcare expenses by exploring advanced preventive care, leveraging technology, understanding billing intricacies, planning for disability, utilizing financing options, engaging with community resources, exploring supplemental income opportunities, and advocating for policy change. This holistic approach not only helps to manage current expenditures but also plans for future healthcare requirements, assuring financial stability and access to high-quality treatment.

Chapter 6: Identifying Additional Income Sources

Exploring new revenue streams is an important technique for increasing financial security and accomplishing long-term financial goals. Whether you want to supplement your primary income, diversify your revenue streams, or save for retirement, having various income sources can provide security and flexibility. This chapter explores several methods for generating additional money, taking into account both traditional and innovative alternatives.

Side hustles and freelancing
People are increasingly turning to side hustles and freelancing to supplement their income. The gig economy provides several options for part-time work that may be adapted to your schedule. Platforms such as Upwork, Fiverr, and TaskRabbit connect freelancers with clients searching for everything from graphic design and writing to handyman jobs and personal

chores. You can generate a consistent source of supplemental income by leveraging your particular skills and knowledge.

Freelancing also gives you more control over your workload and the projects you take on. This flexibility is especially useful for those who have other commitments, such as a full-time employment or family duties. Furthermore, starting a freelance business might lead to bigger opportunities over time, such as higher-paying clients and long-term contracts.

Investing
Investing is an effective approach to increase your wealth and generate extra revenue streams. There are numerous investing possibilities, each with their own risk and return profile. Traditional investments such as stocks, bonds, real estate, and mutual funds can generate passive income in the form of dividends, interest, and capital gains. Understanding the foundations of investing and building a diverse

portfolio can help reduce risks while increasing rewards.

Real estate investing, in particular, provides numerous revenue-generating prospects. Owning rental properties can provide a consistent stream of rental income, and real estate appreciation can result in considerable capital gains over time. Real estate investment trusts (REITs) provide an alternative way to invest in real estate without requiring direct ownership, including dividends and possible value development.

Peer-to-peer lending is another unique investment opportunity in which individuals lend money to others via online platforms while receiving interest on their loans. This strategy can provide larger returns than regular savings accounts, but it also includes more risks.

Passive Income.
Passive income streams demand an initial input of time, money, or both, but produce earnings with little ongoing effort. Passive income can be

defined as royalties from creative works (such as books, music, or patents), rental property income, and investment earnings. Creating digital products, such as e-books or online courses, can also produce passive revenue because they sell over time without requiring further effort.

Building an online profile through blogging, YouTube, or podcasting can result in passive revenue from advertising, sponsorships, and affiliate marketing. These platforms let content creators to monetize their audiences by earning money from advertisements, sponsored content, and commissions for promoting products or services.

Entrepreneurship
Starting your own business is another method to get extra cash. Entrepreneurship has the potential for big financial benefits, but it also carries hazards and demands a significant investment of time and work. Identifying a market need and creating a product or service to meet that

demand can result in a profitable business venture. Whether it's a tiny online store, a consulting firm, or a local service business, entrepreneurship allows you to create a scalable income stream.

E-commerce has made it easier than ever to launch a business with low initial expenditures. Platforms such as Shopify, Etsy, and Amazon enable entrepreneurs to access a worldwide audience and sell their items online. Dropshipping, which allows you to sell things without keeping inventory, lowers the barriers to entry by eliminating the requirement for storage and shipping operations.

Education and Skill Development
Investing in education and skill development can increase your earning potential and lead to new revenue options. Pursuing advanced degrees, certificates, or specialized training might result in higher-paying positions and promotions. Furthermore, learning new skills like coding, digital marketing, or data analysis can qualify

you for freelance jobs or side hustles in high-demand industries.

Continuing education and professional development are critical for remaining competitive in the employment market. Keeping your abilities up to date and relevant increases your chances of landing better-paying jobs and moving up in your profession.

Rental and Sharing Economy
The sharing economy has opened up new revenue streams from unused assets. Renting out a spare room on sites such as Airbnb or Vrbo can provide a significant revenue, particularly in high-demand areas. Similarly, renting out your car, tools, or equipment on sharing economy platforms can convert idle assets into money streams.

Participating in the sharing economy also gives you more flexibility and control over your schedule. You may choose when and how frequently to rent out your assets, making it a convenient option to generate extra money without requiring a major time investment.

Dividend and Interest Income.
Investing in dividend-paying stocks, bonds, and other interest-bearing accounts can generate a consistent income stream. Dividends are payments provided by firms to shareholders, usually quarterly, that reflect a portion of the company's profits. Bondholders receive interest at regular times, resulting in a dependable source of income.

Reinvesting dividends and interest payments can compound your gains over time, improving your earning potential. Dividend reinvestment plans (DRIPs) enable investors to automatically reinvest dividends in new shares of the company's stock, so boosting long-term growth.

The Gig Economy and On-Demand Work
The gig economy provides a wide range of on-demand labor possibilities that can generate extra cash while allowing for flexible hours.

Ride-sharing services like Uber and Lyft, delivery services like DoorDash and Instacart, and freelance platforms all provide multiple opportunities to earn extra money on your own schedule. These options may be particularly tempting to those seeking rapid money without long-term commitments.

On-demand work also allows you to experiment with other professions and industries, gain useful experience, and broaden your professional network. Diversifying your revenue sources through gig economy jobs might help you attain more financial resilience and stability.

Remote work and telecommuting
The rise of remote work and telecommuting has created new earning prospects for those looking for extra money sources. Many companies provide part-time or freelance remote job opportunities, allowing you to earn money from the comfort of your own home. Remote work opportunities include customer service, virtual assistance, content development, and IT support.

Remote work also allows you to handle various revenue sources at the same time because you may balance different tasks and responsibilities without being limited by the limits of a regular workplace. This flexibility might result in a more diverse and reliable income portfolio.

Government Programs and Grants
Exploring government programs and grants can give financial assistance for a variety of efforts, including launching a business and pursuing education or research projects. Many government agencies provide grants and financial options to small firms, entrepreneurs, and individuals looking to better their professions. Researching and applying for these programs can help you generate revenue.

Finally, looking for new ways to earn money requires a diverse approach that takes advantage of your abilities, assets, and possibilities. You can diversify and strengthen your income portfolio by doing side hustles, freelancing, investing, entrepreneurship, continuing education, the sharing economy, dividend and interest income, the gig economy, remote work, and participating in government programs. This complete strategy not only improves your financial stability, but it also gives you the freedom and resources you need to meet your long-term financial objectives.

Exploring new revenue streams is a constant process that involves ingenuity, patience, and a willingness to adapt to new opportunities. One method for creating extra income is to use your existing professional network to seek out consulting or advising opportunities. Many sectors value seasoned experts' skills and ideas, so working as a consultant can be a profitable way to contribute your knowledge and experience. This not only gives cash rewards, but it also allows you to remain active in your area and build professional ties.

Another option to examine is the development and commercialization of intellectual property. This could include creating software, apps, or other digital items to meet unique requirements or challenges. The rise of app stores and online marketplaces has made it easier to distribute and sell digital products. Once the original creation is completed, intellectual property can produce ongoing income through sales, licensing agreements, or subscription models, resulting in a consistent cash stream with minimal upkeep.

Participating in community-based economic activities can also be a good way to earn extra money. Local markets, fairs, and community events provide opportunities to sell handmade, craft, or artisanal products. Participating in these events can help you gain local customers and foster a sense of community connection. Furthermore, working with other local entrepreneurs can result in mutually beneficial relationships and the sharing of resources and information.

Educational platforms provide several chances for those who enjoy teaching and mentoring to supplement their income. You can produce and sell online courses through platforms such as Udemy or Coursera, as well as provide private teaching and coaching sessions. Sharing your knowledge on topics ranging from academics to hobbies and talents can attract a wide audience and provide a meaningful method to earn money while helping others reach their goals.

Exploring income prospects in financial markets is another option. Trading stocks, options, or cryptocurrency can result in substantial rewards, but it also carries more risk. Successful trading requires a deep understanding of market dynamics, technical analysis, and risk management. Participating in investment clubs or communities can bring useful insights and assistance from other traders.

Furthermore, understanding the possibilities of worldwide marketplaces will help you increase your earning opportunities. With the capacity to work and sell items or services online, you are no longer limited to your local area. This global view can lead to new consumer bases and revenue streams. Offering language translation services, exporting products, or entering international freelance marketplaces can all help to diversify your income and reduce the risks associated with relying on a single market.

Leveraging the power of social media and digital marketing can also boost your earnings potential. Building a strong online presence on sites such as Instagram, Twitter, and LinkedIn can lead to new business opportunities, sponsorships, and collaborations. Effective social media marketing can attract traffic to your products or services while also increasing sales. Furthermore, connecting with your audience and delivering valuable material can help you position yourself as an authority in your niche, opening up new revenue options.

Another technique to increase your earnings is through strategic financial planning and optimization. Regularly assessing and altering your financial plans, such as optimising your tax situation, refinancing debt, or taking advantage of employer advantages, can free up extra funds that can be reinvested or utilized to produce more income. Working with a financial advisor can provide individualized insights and recommendations based on your specific financial circumstances.

It is also worth exploring franchising as a means of generating additional revenue. Investing in a franchise can provide a complete company model that includes proven branding, marketing, and operational systems. This can be an appealing choice for those wishing to enter a proven company model with the support of a franchisor. Conducting comprehensive study and selecting a franchise that matches your interests and skills can result in a successful and profitable company.

Furthermore, participating in humanitarian activities can indirectly increase your earnings potential. Volunteering, serving on nonprofit boards, or participating in humanitarian activities can help you extend your network, learn new skills, and improve your reputation. These activities can lead to new opportunities, partnerships, and business endeavors, as well as provide personal fulfillment and communal benefit.

Chapter 7: Staying Active and Engaged.

Staying active and engaged is critical for leading a meaningful and vibrant life, especially as you age or enter retirement. Physical activity, social interaction, and cerebral stimulation are all important factors in maintaining overall well-being and quality of life. This chapter delves into many strategies to keep active and involved, highlighting the advantages of a comprehensive approach to health and happiness.

The Importance of Physical Activity
Regular physical activity is essential for overall health, preventing chronic diseases, and improving mental wellness. Exercise promotes cardiovascular health, strengthens muscles and bones, and improves flexibility and balance. This is especially crucial as we age, as it reduces the likelihood of falls and injuries. Exercise also causes the release of endorphins, which are

natural mood enhancers that aid in the treatment of stress, anxiety, and sadness.

There are numerous types of physical activity to suit different tastes and fitness levels. Walking, jogging, swimming, and cycling are all great cardiovascular exercises that may be readily included into regular routines. Strength training exercises, such as lifting weights or utilizing resistance bands, aid in the maintenance of muscle mass and bone density. Flexibility exercises, such as yoga and stretching, improve mobility and lower the chance of injury. Group fitness activities, such as aerobics, dancing, and Pilates, offer social connection and encouragement while keeping you active.

Participating in sports and recreational activities can also be an enjoyable method to maintain physical fitness. Tennis, golf, hiking, and other sports not only bring physical benefits, but they also allow you to socialize and make new acquaintances. Exploring local parks, nature trails, and community centers can lead to a range of activities that will keep you active and involved.

Social Engagement and Community Involvement
Maintaining social activity is also vital for general well-being. Social relationships improve emotional health, establish support networks, and foster a sense of belonging. Engaging with family, friends, and community members helps to reduce feelings of isolation and loneliness, which can have a severe influence on both mental and physical health.

Volunteering is a meaningful way to keep socially involved while also contributing to the community. Many organizations, including charities, schools, hospitals, and animal shelters, rely on volunteers to fulfill their purposes. Volunteering not only helps others, but also gives you a sense of purpose and fulfillment. It can connect you with new people, broaden your social circle, and provide opportunity to master new skills.

Joining clubs, groups, or organizations based on common interests is another efficient approach to maintain social activity. Book clubs, gardening groups, travel clubs, and interest organizations all offer regular opportunities for contact and participation. Participating in local events such as cultural festivals, fairs, and community gatherings promotes social relationships and enriches your social life.

Lifelong Learning and Mental Stimulation
Continuous learning and mental stimulation are essential for preserving cognitive health and avoiding cognitive decline. Engaging in intellectually engaging activities keeps the brain busy and helps boost memory, problem-solving abilities, and creativity. Developing new knowledge and abilities can boost your sense of accomplishment and self-esteem.

There are several techniques to maintain mental activity and engagement. Reading books, newspapers, and magazines helps you stay informed and introduces you to fresh ideas and perspectives. Enrolling in courses or workshops at local community colleges, universities, or online platforms allows you to learn about things you are interested in, such as languages, history, technology, and the arts. Online learning sites such as Coursera, edX, and Khan Academy provide a diverse choice of courses that can be accessed from the convenience of your own home.

Puzzles, chess, and strategic games are all examples of mentally stimulating hobbies. Creative hobbies like painting, writing, or playing a musical instrument promote cognitive flexibility and expressiveness. Participating in discussion groups or debate clubs improves critical thinking abilities and allows for intellectual connection with others.

Promoting a Positive Mindset and Emotional Wellbeing

Maintaining a healthy mindset and emotional well-being is critical for a satisfying life. Mindfulness and stress management strategies like meditation, deep breathing, and yoga can help you stay grounded and resilient in the face of adversity. Focusing on thankfulness and positive thinking might help you improve your view on life and feel happier overall.

Building strong emotional bonds with loved ones is essential for emotional well-being. Open communication, empathy, and quality time with family and friends all help to deepen these ties and give a support system during difficult times. Seeking professional help, such as counseling or therapy, can help you manage your mental health and navigate life transitions.

Exploring New Opportunities and Adventures

Staying involved frequently entails moving outside of your comfort zone and seeking new chances and experiences. Traveling to new areas, whether locally or globally, broadens your perspective and exposes you to new cultures and experiences. Travel can provide inspiration, leisure, and opportunities for personal growth.

Trying new hobbies and following long-held interests can provide excitement and a sense of accomplishment. Whether you're learning to cook new foods, taking up photography, or participating in adventure sports, these experiences enrich your life and offer limitless prospects for exploration and enjoyment.

Creating a Balanced and Active Lifestyle
A balanced and active lifestyle entails incorporating physical activity, social interaction, cerebral stimulation, and emotional well-being into your daily routine. Setting attainable goals and creating a schedule that includes time for exercise, social engagement, learning, and relaxation contributes to a well-rounded lifestyle. Flexibility is also vital, as

it allows you to adapt to new activities and interests as they emerge.

Engaging with nature and spending time outside can be beneficial to both physical and mental health. Activities such as gardening, hiking, or simply going for a walk in the park provide fresh air, natural beauty, and a break from daily life.

Staying active and involved is essential for living a meaningful life, and it includes a variety of activities that excite the body, mind, and soul. Beyond typical tactics, there are creative and frequently neglected ways to increase your engagement and activity levels.

One such way is to incorporate awareness into everyday activities. Mindfulness, or the practice of being present and completely involved in the moment, may turn mundane tasks into opportunities for relaxation and mental clarity. Simple practices such as mindful walking, where you focus on the sensations of each step, and mindful eating, where you chew each piece and notice the aromas and textures, can improve ordinary activities while also reducing stress.

Engaging in creative activities can greatly improve your mental and emotional health. Painting, sculpting, and crafts are all examples of therapeutic activities that allow people to express themselves and reduce stress. They also give you a sense of success and joy because you're creating something unique and personalized. Journaling, poetry, and storytelling are all forms of creative writing that allow you to explore your thoughts and feelings while also providing insight and emotional relief.

Cultural participation is yet another effective way to keep active and stimulated. Attending theatrical shows, concerts, art exhibits, or literary readings might help you learn new things and be creative. Participating in cultural festivals or events not only broadens your horizons, but also builds a stronger bond with your town and its various forms of art and heritage.

Travel, particularly experiential travel, has the potential to significantly increase your level of involvement. Instead of usual tourist activities, look for immersive experiences that allow you to interact with local cultures and traditions. This could include staying with local families, taking traditional crafts or cooking workshops, or working on community service initiatives. Such encounters provide in-depth insights into various ways of living while also promoting personal growth and understanding.

Engaging with nature in more meaningful ways can boost your vitality and connection to the environment. Forest bathing, a Japanese technique that involves immersing oneself in the forest environment, has been demonstrated to relieve stress and promote mental health. Spending time in nature, whether hiking, camping, or simply sitting by a river, may bring tremendous calm and refreshment.

Learning new talents, especially those that challenge you in unique ways, can help you stay cognitively bright and interested. This could involve learning a new language, which improves cognitive performance while also providing new cultural and social opportunities. Taking up a musical instrument can be both mentally engaging and emotionally fulfilling, giving you a creative outlet and a sense of achievement as you grow.

Intergenerational partnerships can offer distinct benefits and perspectives. Mentoring younger people or volunteering in schools and youth organizations allows you to offer your knowledge and experience while making meaningful relationships and growing together. These interactions can be extremely rewarding and assist to overcome generational barriers, boosting understanding and cooperation.

For people interested in advocacy and activism, volunteering for social causes can be a great way to stay active and make a difference. Whether it's environmental protection, social justice, or public health, volunteering for issues you care about can help you feel a sense of purpose and community. This involvement can take numerous forms, including marching and rallying, organizing community events, and collaborating with charities.

Spiritual activities can also play an important role in maintaining engagement and fulfillment. Exploring various spiritual or philosophical traditions can help you gain deeper insights into your beliefs and values, as well as a stronger feeling of purpose and connection. Meditation, prayer, and attending religious or spiritual meetings can all provide comfort, camaraderie, and a sense of connection.

Finally, pursuing lifelong learning through a variety of educational options helps keep your mind busy and engaged. This could include attending lectures, joining discussion groups, or participating in online forums where you can debate and study a variety of themes. Engaging with new and challenging ideas keeps your mind active, which can lead to personal and intellectual progress.

Staying active and involved requires a comprehensive approach that encompasses many facets of life. You can have a rich and fulfilling life by pursuing mindfulness, creativity, cultural engagement, experiential travel, nature, new skills, intergenerational relationships, activism, spiritual practices, and lifelong learning. These activities not only improve your physical, mental, and emotional health, but they also give you a feeling of purpose, connection, and joy, which improves your entire life.

Conclusion

Conclusion: Your Path to a Secure and Happy Retirement

Reaching a secure and happy retirement is more than just a financial goal—it's a profound journey that combines careful planning, informed decisions, and a proactive approach to managing your resources. As you've discovered throughout Proven Ways to Make Your Money Last, achieving financial stability is within your grasp with the right strategies and mindset.

This book has equipped you with the tools and knowledge to:

- **Set Clear Goals**: Define what a successful retirement looks like for you and create a roadmap to get there.
- **Build a Robust Budget**: Manage your income and expenses effectively to ensure sustainability and flexibility.

- **Invest Wisely**: Make informed investment choices that balance risk and reward, tailored to your individual needs.
- **Optimize Taxes**: Navigate the complexities of tax laws to maximize your savings and minimize liabilities.
- **Manage Healthcare Costs**: Plan for medical expenses and insurance to avoid financial surprises.
- **Generate Additional Income**: Explore various income streams to supplement your retirement fund and maintain your lifestyle.
- **Stay Active and Engaged**: Embrace a vibrant and fulfilling retirement by staying involved in activities that enrich your life.

Remember, the journey to a secure and happy retirement is ongoing. Continue to educate yourself, stay adaptable, and be proactive in making decisions that benefit your long-term financial health. Your future is shaped by the actions you take today, and with the insights from this book, you are well-prepared to navigate the path ahead.

As you move forward, let the principles and strategies outlined in this book be your guide. Embrace the opportunities and challenges with confidence, knowing that you have the tools to make your money last and to enjoy the retirement you've always envisioned.

Here's to a future filled with security, peace of mind, and the freedom to live your retirement years to the fullest.

....

Notes..

Notes..

....

www.ingramcontent.com/pod-product-compliance
Lightning Source LLC
Chambersburg PA
CBHW050312230526
45471CB00005B/2144